HOW TO MANAGE YOUR PERSONAL KNOWLEDGE

How to Manage Your Personal Knowledge

Pralhad Jadhav

First Printing, 2025

Contents

Dedication

This book is dedicated to my mother Shanta Ramchandra Jadhav. It is through her eyes that I first saw the world, and through her values that I learned to live with grace, compassion, and courage. Whatever I am today is a reflection of the light she placed within me.

Acknowledgement

This book would never have seen the light of day if Mr. Manoj Sonawane had not persuaded me to write it. His support extended far beyond that. He played a vital role in launching and promoting the book on global platforms. I remain deeply grateful for his unwavering support, guidance, and belief in this journey.

I extend my heartfelt gratitude to the BLISS Books Editorial Team for skillfully transforming my raw ideas into refined, meaningful wisdom.

On the professional front, I am especially thankful to my friend, Prof. Sandeep Bhavsar, whose insights and experiences have consistently offered me fresh direction and inspiration.

I am thankful to Mr. Chetan Taksale, whose guidance and insights have greatly benefited me in my professional journey.

Above all, I am deeply grateful to my mentors and guides, Prof. Rajendra Kumbhar and Prof. Yathan, whose wisdom and mentorship have left a lasting impact on my journey.

I would also like to express my heartfelt gratitude to my firm, Khaitan & Co, India's premier law firm. The values and professional environment at Khaitan & Co have deeply influenced my personal and intellectual growth, and have been a silent yet significant source of inspiration throughout this journey."

Love and Gratitude
Mr. Pralhad Jadhav

Foreword

We live in an age of unprecedented information abundance and exhaustion. Yet, despite this digital torrent, we often feel overwhelmed and confused, unable to turn all this information into useful knowledge. The real challenge today isn't finding information but knowing how to harness and use it wisely.

This is where Pralhad Jadhav's *How to Manage Your Personal Knowledge: Wisdom for Creating a Second Brain* arrives as a lighthouse. Drawing from decades of expertise in library science and knowledge management, Mr. Jadhav invites us on a transformative journey, one that turns scattered knowledge into structured intelligence and passive consumption into creative contribution.

What sets this book apart is its profound practicality. Jadhav avoids abstract theories, instead offering actionable frameworks like the PARA Method, Zettelkasten, and Digital Gardens tools that transform scattered ideas into interconnected, retrievable insights. He recognizes that knowledge management isn't just for corporations or academics; it's essential for students, professionals, artists, and lifelong learners alike. Whether you're a librarian curating resources, a writer synthesizing research, or a student battling information overload, this book equips you to build a resilient "second brain": an external system that amplifies your creativity, clarity, and capacity for growth.

Jadhav's approach is holistic. He doesn't just teach you what tools to use; he reveals how to think about knowledge itself, distinguishing data from information, information from wisdom, and activity from impact. Through relatable case studies (like Shaheen's tacit knowledge in libraries or Sarah's digital literacy journey), he demonstrates that PKM is both an art and a science, deeply human yet enhanced by technology. By the final pages, Mr. Jadhav shows us how to build a "second brain", a dynamic, digital extension of our own minds.

To read this book is to invest in your greatest asset: your attention. Let it transform how you learn, create, and ultimately, how you shape a meaningful life in the knowledge economy.

Manoj Sonawane

Author of the book Learning 2.0 | Knowledgepreneur | Book Strategist | Mentor to Visionary Authors

1

Introduction

Did you have any idea that in just one day, the average person today is exposed to the same amount of information as someone in the 15th century would encounter in their entire lifetime? It's mind-boggling, isn't it? Thanks to the internet and digital technology, we now find ourselves drowning in an overwhelming flood of knowledge and data. It's a lot to handle, to say the least. That's why effectively managing and organizing this information has never been more crucial.

In my book titled "How to Manage Your Personal Knowledge: Wisdom for Creating a Second Brain," we delve deep into the captivating and expansive realm of personal knowledge management. This exploration will highlight not only its importance but also its profound implications for various stakeholders, including librarians, library users, and those in pursuit of knowledge. By examining the dynamics and strategies involved in effectively managing personal knowledge, we aim to uncover the invaluable benefits that this approach offers to individuals who seek to enhance their understanding and organization of information.

Personal knowledge management, or PKM for short, refers to the strategies and tools individuals employ to acquire, organize, store, and retrieve information for their personal and professional growth. In our fast-paced, information-rich society, the ability to effectively manage our personal knowledge has become a vital skill.

But why are we focusing on the perspective of library users and librarians as well, you ask? Well, libraries have always been at the forefront of knowledge management. Librarians are seasoned professionals who have dedicated their careers to organizing and disseminating information. They fully grasp the significance of effective knowledge management and can provide invaluable insights and strategies for users to enhance their own PKM practices.

Throughout the pages of this book, we'll explore a multitude of topics ranging from information overload and digital literacy to information retrieval and knowledge organization. Additionally, we'll delve into the challenges faced by librarians, library users, or knowledge seekers in managing personal knowledge in our increasingly digital world.

What's more, we'll showcase real-life examples and case studies from libraries and individuals who have successfully implemented PKM strategies. These examples will serve as inspiration and guidance for readers as they develop their own personalized knowledge management systems.

So, whether you're a knowledge seekers looking to enhance your information management skills or a librarian seeking to elevate your services and support for patrons, this book is for you. It's a comprehensive guide that brings together theoretical frameworks, practical advice, and innovative ideas to help you navigate the intricate landscape of personal knowledge management.

Don't let information overload overwhelm you. Take control of your knowledge and unleash it to its full potential. Let's embark on this exhilarating journey together.

2

Types of Knowledge Management

****

*"The organization of information actually creates new information." - **Richard Saul Wurman***

There are two types of knowledge management: Tacit knowledge management and explicit knowledge management. Let's learn more about it in this chapter.

Knowledge Management is an art form that involves the systematic management of an organization's intellectual goldmine. It encompasses a plethora of processes, strategies, and techniques that enable the creation, sharing, and utilization of knowledge to achieve organizational goals and elevate performance. In this chapter, we'll dive headfirst into these two types of knowledge management and how they play a pivotal role in personal knowledge management (PKM) by using the story of Shaheen.

To bring you an authentic perspective on knowledge management, we have the privilege of hearing from Shaheen, a seasoned librarian with over a decade of experience in a bustling college library. Throughout her career, Shaheen has witnessed the profound impact of effective knowledge management both in her role as a librarian and in serving library-goers. Her wisdom and experiences will illuminate the practical side of knowledge management in the context of a library.

Shaheen's captivating narrative commences with her encounters in managing tacit knowledge. Tacit knowledge, an elusive form of wisdom, is not easily codified or documented. It is deeply personal, rooted in an individual's mastery, expertise, and intuition. Shaheen will regale us with tales of how she has deftly wielded tacit knowledge in her work, such as crafting tailor-made recommendations for patrons based on their unique interests and needs. She deep dive into the challenges she has encountered in managing this enigmatic knowledge, such as capturing it and sharing it with her colleagues.

Transitioning seamlessly, Shaheen shifts gears to explore the realm of explicit knowledge management. Unlike its elusive counterpart, explicit knowledge is the structured and formal knowledge that can be easily documented and transferred. Shaheen grace us with her experiences in organizing and categorizing information, building knowledge repositories, and establishing tried-and-true procedures and guidelines for library operations. She expound upon the virtues of explicit knowledge management in fostering consistency, streamlining operations, and encouraging knowledge sharing among the library staff.

After laying the groundwork with her testimonial on tacit knowledge management, Shaheen unravels how tacit knowledge is the lifeblood of the personalized and intuitive service that librarians provide. She also addresses the hurdles of effectively capturing and sharing this invaluable knowledge. She explores various strategies and tools that can aid in the management of tacit knowledge, such as mentoring programs and vibrant communities of practice.

Shaheen concludes her reflections by examining the significance of explicit knowledge management in the library environment. She dissects the advantages of organizing and documenting knowledge, such as ensuring unwavering consistency and facilitating seamless knowledge transfer. However, she also shines a light on the potential pitfalls of solely relying on explicit knowledge, such as overlooking the intangible beauty of tacit knowledge and the inherent limitations of codified information. Shaheen eloquently argues for the necessity of a harmonious blend of both tacit and explicit knowledge management strategies.

By embarking on a journey through Shaheen's experiences and insights, we have peeled back the layers of different knowledge management approaches. This chapter serves as a treasured resource for library and professionals alike, deepening their understanding of how knowledge management can enrich their educational escapades and elevate their professional prowess.

In the next chapter, we'll discuss about how knowledge management differs from personal knowledge management. This exploration will highlight the unique characteristics and implementations of each, allowing for a clearer understanding of how they diverge from one another.

Action Points:

1. Identify Tacit Knowledge: List 3 skills you possess that are hard to document (e.g., intuitive problem-solving).
2. Capture Explicit Knowledge: Document one work process step-by-step in a shared tool (Google Docs/ Notion).
3. Interview a Mentor: Ask a colleague how they transfer tacit knowledge (e.g., through storytelling or shadowing).

3

KM Versus PKM

****

"Knowledge is like paint... it does no good until it is applied."
- Doe Zantamata

Knowledge Management (KM) is the systematic process of capturing, distributing, and effectively using knowledge within an organization. It's all about identifying, creating, organizing, and sharing information and expertise to improve decision-making, problem-solving, and innovation. Basically, it's the secret sauce to success for any company or organization.

But wait, there's more! Personal Knowledge Management (PKM) takes it a step further, honing in on how individuals gather, classify, store, search, retrieve, and share knowledge in their day-to-day activities. Think of it as a personal knowledge assistant, helping you become a rockstar in your personal, academic, and professional pursuits by keeping everything in order.

Now, let's talk advantages. The benefits of knowledge management are numerous for organizations. It's like a magic wand that allows them to tap into the collective knowledge of their team, achieving goals like nobody's business. It also sparks innovation, promotes collaboration, and makes them more competitive. Need proof? Look no further than Google and Microsoft, two companies that have harnessed KM strategies to boost productivity, squash duplication of efforts, and solve problems at lightning speed.

But hold on, individuals aren't left out in the cold. PKM is a game-changer for them too. It turbocharges productivity by giving them instant access to the information they need, when they need it. It fuels creativity by connecting seemingly unrelated ideas. And it helps them make better decisions by providing a solid knowledge foundation. Just ask any professional in a creative field like design or writing – they'll tell you that tools like Evernote and OneNote are their secret weapons for capturing and organizing their genius ideas and inspiration.

But alas, like all good things, there are challenges and downsides. For KM, one hurdle is capturing that elusive tacit knowledge – the stuff that's locked away inside people's heads and is a pain to put into words. Then there's information overload, which makes it harder than finding a needle in a haystack to uncover the knowledge that actually matters. Xerox learned this the hard way with their failed attempt at KM, thanks to cultural barriers, lack of leadership support, and a less-than-stellar technology infrastructure.

And PKM? It has its own set of obstacles. Information overload is just as big of a headache for individuals trying to manage their knowledge. With so much info at their fingertips, it's like drinking from a firehose – overwhelming and hard to filter. Then there's the issue of maintaining consistency. Personal knowledge repositories can be a bit all over the place, lacking standardized structures. And let's not forget the time and effort it takes for individuals to manage their own knowledge. It's no walk in the park.

So, what's the difference between KM and PKM? KM is all about collective knowledge management within organizations, focusing on collaboration and standardization. It's like a symphony, bringing everyone together to play in harmony. On the other hand, PKM is all about individual knowledge management, letting people do their own thing and dance to their own beat. It's perfect for those who want to maximize personal productivity and keep their knowledge organized.

At the end of the day, whether you choose KM or PKM depends on your specific needs, goals, and context. If you're an organization looking to foster collaboration, standardize processes, and tap into collective knowledge, KM is your jam. But if you're an individual or a small group craving personal productivity, creativity, and individual learning, PKM is where it's at. Or, why not have the best of both worlds? A little bit of KM and a little bit of PKM can create the ultimate knowledge management strategy that's tailor-made for your unique needs.

In the next chapter, let's take a closer look at how we can enhance and refine our personal knowledge management journey by diving deeper into the distinctions and relationships between Data, Information, and Knowledge. Understanding these concepts will provide a clearer framework for organizing and managing what you learn and how you apply your insights effectively.

Action Points:

1. Audit Your Tools: List apps you use for personal (PKM) vs. team (KM) knowledge. Delete one redundant tool.
2. Solve a Problem: Use your personal notes to resolve a work challenge within 24 hours.
3. Share One Insight: Post a key takeaway from this chapter on LinkedIn or an internal team chat.

4

Foundations of Personal Knowledge Management

****

"Knowledge is power, but only when it's organized and accessible." - ***Peter Drucker***

Data vs. Information vs. Knowledge:

Comprehending the fundamental principles of Knowledge Management (KM) and Personal Knowledge Management (PKM) necessitates a precise and thorough distinction among the key foundational components, which include data, information, and knowledge-and an exploration of how these concepts interplay to form the basis of effective knowledge systems.

It's a crucial aspect of PKM in understanding how raw data transforms into actionable knowledge. Let's distinguish them here:

1. Data: The Raw Material

Data is the most basic unit in the hierarchy of understanding. It is raw, unprocessed, and often lacks meaning or context. Data points are the building blocks from which information and knowledge are derived.

Characteristics of Data:

- Raw and unstructured.
- Independent of interpretation.
- Often quantitative or qualitative.
- Context-free, making it difficult to interpret on its own.

Examples:

- Temperature readings: 72°F, 75°F, 78°F.
- Sales figures: $5,000, $7,200, $6,800.
- Individual words in a text: red, car, fast.

2. Information: Adding Context

Information emerges when data is processed, organized, and contextualized. It answers questions like "who," "what," "where," and "when." While information is more meaningful than data, it still requires interpretation to provide value.

Characteristics of Information:

- Organized and structured.
- Provides context to raw data.
- Can be shared and communicated more easily.

Examples:

- A weather report stating: The temperature in New York rose from 72°F to 78°F over three hours.
- A sales summary: Revenue increased by 20% compared to last month.
- A sentence: The red car sped past the finish line.

3. Knowledge: The Actionable Insight

Knowledge is the synthesis of information through analysis, experience, and application. It represents the "how" and "why" behind facts, providing actionable insights for decision-making and problem-solving.

Characteristics of Knowledge:

- Derived from experience, education, and analysis.
- Contextual, actionable, and adaptable.
- Enables decision-making and problem-solving.

Examples:

- Understanding weather patterns to predict storms.
- Using sales trends to forecast future revenue.
- Knowing how to drive a car and adjust speeds appropriately.

The Data-Information-Knowledge Continuum

The transformation from data to knowledge is not automatic; it involves deliberate processing, analysis, and critical thinking. This continuum can be visualized as follows:

Collection: Raw data is gathered from various sources, such as sensors, reports, or observations.

Processing: Data is organized and structured to create information. This might involve sorting, categorizing, or applying basic analysis.

Understanding: Through reflection, analysis, and experience, information evolves into knowledge.

For instance, in the context of health monitoring:

Data: A fitness tracker records heart rates throughout the day.

Information: An app organizes these readings into a chart showing daily activity patterns.

Knowledge: A fitness expert interprets the patterns to suggest a workout plan tailored to the individual's heart health.

The Importance of Personal Knowledge Management

In today's digital era, where data and information abound, effective PKM is indispensable. With the right strategies and tools, individuals can filter overwhelming information streams and focus on meaningful insights to enhance productivity and decision-making.

Key Benefits of PKM:

Enhanced Productivity: Streamlined access to relevant knowledge reduces wasted time.

Informed Decision-Making: Actionable insights lead to better personal and professional choices.

Continuous Learning: PKM fosters lifelong learning by encouraging the systematic acquisition and application of knowledge.

Improved Collaboration: Organized personal knowledge makes sharing ideas with others more effective.

Having explored the roots of knowledge management (KM) and personal knowledge management (PKM), and how raw data blossoms into valuable knowledge, let's shift our focus.

In the upcoming chapter, we'll equip ourselves with practical tools to effectively manage this valuable knowledge.

Action Points:

1. Transform Data: Convert raw data (e.g., daily screen time) into actionable insight (e.g., "Reduce social media by 30 mins").
2. Apply Feynman Technique: Explain a complex concept in simple terms to a friend. Note gaps in your understanding.
3. Create a "Knowledge Recipe": Template: "When I see [DATA], I convert it to [INFORMATION] by [ACTION], resulting in [KNOWLEDGE]."

5

Tools and Application for PKM

****

"Knowledge is power. Sharing knowledge is the key to unlocking that power." - ***Martin Uzochukwu Ugwu***

In the age of information, we are constantly bombarded with data from multiple sources—emails, social media, books, articles, videos, and conversations. While this wealth of information is invaluable, it can also be overwhelming without a system to manage, organize, and retrieve it efficiently. It needs efficient tools and techniques to streamline this information. Here, we will explore strategies to build an effective PKM system, empowering you to turn scattered information into actionable insights.

Understand Your Objectives

Before diving into tools and techniques, clarify why you want to manage your knowledge effectively. Are you looking to:

- Improve productivity at work?
- Enhance personal learning and skill development?
- Organize information for creative projects?
- Build a repository for future reference?

Having clear objectives will help you choose the right tools and strategies for your needs.

Adopt a Reliable Framework

A structured framework provides a roadmap for managing knowledge. One popular model is Tiago Forte's PARA Method, which organizes information into four categories:

- **Projects:** Active tasks or initiatives you're working on.
- **Areas:** Long-term responsibilities (e.g., health, finances, relationships).
- **Resources:** Reference materials for ongoing or future interests.
- **Archive:** Information you want to keep but no longer need actively.

This system allows for efficient categorization, ensuring that all information has its place.

Capture Information Effectively

The first step in PKM is capturing knowledge as it comes to you. To do this effectively:

• **Use a Digital Inbox:** Apps like Evernote, Notion, or Obsidian can serve as central repositories for notes, links, and ideas.

• **Leverage Mobile Tools:** Mobile apps let you capture fleeting thoughts or information on the go.

• **Embrace Voice Notes:** For moments when typing isn't practical, voice memos can be invaluable.

The key is to capture ideas immediately, preventing valuable insights from slipping through the cracks.

Organize Information Intuitively

An effective PKM system relies on an intuitive structure that makes information easy to retrieve. Consider the following techniques:

• **Tagging:** Use descriptive tags to make searching for information quicker and more precise.

• **Folders or Databases:** Group related content into folders or databases for better categorization.

• **Mind Maps:** Tools like MindMeister or XMind allow you to visually organize ideas and connect related concepts.

Keep your structure simple to minimize friction when adding or retrieving information.

Use Tools Wisely

The right tools can significantly enhance your PKM process. Here are some options:

• **Note-Taking Apps:** Obsidian, Notion, or Roam Research for capturing and organizing thoughts.

• **Task Managers:** Tools like Todoist or Microsoft To Do for tracking actionable tasks.

• **Bookmark Managers:** Save and organize web resources with tools like Pocket or Raindrop.io.

• **Cloud Storage:** Services like Google Drive or Dropbox for storing larger files and documents.

Choose tools that integrate well with each other to avoid duplication and maximize efficiency.

Regularly Review and Update

Information that isn't reviewed or updated regularly can quickly become irrelevant. Schedule time for:

• **Weekly Reviews**: Revisit notes, tasks, and projects to ensure everything is up-to-date.

• **Monthly Cleanups**: Archive outdated material and reorganize your database for clarity.

• **Annual Audits:** Evaluate your entire PKM system to identify what works, what doesn't, and what needs adjustment.

Consistent maintenance prevents your system from becoming cluttered.

Practice Active Reading and Note-Taking

When consuming information, active engagement is critical. Here's how:

• **Highlight Key Points:** Use tools like Kindle Highlights or browser extensions for digital texts.

• **Annotate:** Add personal thoughts, questions, or summaries to deepen your understanding.

• **Summarize:** Write brief summaries to distill essential insights and make them easier to review.

Active reading transforms passive consumption into actionable learning.

Build Connections Between Ideas

The true power of PKM lies in connecting disparate pieces of information to generate new insights. This can be achieved through:

- **Linked Notes:** Tools like Obsidian or Roam Research allow for interlinking notes, creating a "knowledge graph."
- **Concept Mapping:** Explore relationships between ideas visually with mind mapping tools.
- **Zettelkasten Method:** This technique involves linking notes using unique IDs, enabling you to build a web of interconnected ideas.

The ability to see patterns and connections can lead to creative breakthroughs and deeper understanding.

Focus on Outputs

While capturing and organizing are critical, the ultimate goal of PKM is to produce meaningful outputs. Whether it's a project, a report, or a creative endeavor, use your knowledge repository to:

- **Solve Problems:** Apply insights to tackle challenges effectively.
- **Teach Others:** Writing blog posts, creating videos, or sharing summaries helps solidify your understanding.
- **Create Content:** Use your knowledge base as inspiration for creative work.

Producing outputs ensures that your PKM efforts yield tangible benefits.

Automate Where Possible

Automation reduces manual effort and enhances efficiency. Consider automating:

- **Note Syncing:** Use apps that synchronize across devices.
- **Task Management:** Link tools like Evernote or Notion with task managers to create reminders.
- **Information Capture:** Use browser extensions or RSS feeds to collect updates from your favorite sources.

Automation allows you to focus on higher-value activities.

Balance Digital and Analog

While digital tools dominate modern PKM, analog methods like journals or physical notebooks can complement them. Writing by hand can enhance memory retention and provide a distraction-free environment for deep thinking. Consider using a hybrid approach to get the best of both worlds.

Stay Consistent

A PKM system is only as good as your commitment to using it. Establish daily habits for capturing and organizing information. For example:

- Spend 10 minutes each morning reviewing tasks and priorities.

• Dedicate time each evening to jot down insights or organize new material.

Consistency ensures your PKM system evolves with you and remains a reliable resource.

Embrace Minimalism

It's tempting to collect every piece of information you come across, but this can lead to clutter. Adopt a minimalist mindset by:

• **Focusing on Quality Over Quantity:** Save only the most relevant or impactful information.

• **Deleting Redundant Data:** Regularly prune unnecessary notes or files.

• **Limiting Tools:** Avoid using too many apps that duplicate functionality.

A streamlined system is easier to manage and less overwhelming.

Collaborate and Share

PKM isn't just a solitary activity. Collaborating with others can provide fresh perspectives and foster knowledge exchange. Join communities or participate in discussions related to your field. Sharing your insights not only helps others but also reinforces your understanding.

Measure Success

Periodically assess whether your PKM system is helping you achieve your goals. Ask yourself:

• Are you retrieving information quickly and efficiently?

• Are you producing better work or solving problems more effectively?

• Are you staying organized and reducing stress?

Adjust your approach based on these reflections to ensure continuous improvement.

Effective Personal Knowledge Management is a powerful tool for navigating the complexities of the modern information landscape. By adopting a structured approach, leveraging the right tools, and maintaining consistent habits, you can transform scattered information into a valuable resource that supports your learning, creativity, and productivity.

PKM is not a one-size-fits-all solution. It's a personal journey that evolves with your needs and objectives. Start small, experiment with different strategies, and build a system that works for you. Over time, you'll find that managing your knowledge effectively becomes second nature, enabling you to achieve more with greater clarity and confidence.

In the next chapter, we will examine the strategies for managing personal knowledge effectively.

Action Points:

1. Set Up a Digital Inbox: Install Obsidian/Evernote. Capture 10 ideas/tasks this week.
2. Tag Existing Notes: Apply 3 descriptive tags (e.g., #ProjectX, #Urgent) to old notes.

3. Automate One Task: Use Zapier/IFFT to auto-save email attachments to Google Drive.

6

Strategies for Effective PKM

****

"Measure not just what you store, but what you create. Your output is the truest metric of knowledge mastery."- **Unknown**

Effective Personal Knowledge Management requires setting clear goals, prioritizing them, managing time and tasks effectively. These practices not only enhance productivity but also foster personal and professional growth. Let's learn about it in detail in this chapter.

Goal Setting and Prioritization in Personal Knowledge Management

Setting and prioritizing goals can significantly impact Personal Knowledge Management (PKM). It is the foundation of effective PKM, providing a clear direction and purpose for knowledge acquisition. When our goals align with our personal and professional objectives, the knowledge we acquire becomes more meaningful and valuable. Let's learn how to implement this strategy below.

To set goals effectively in PKM, it's crucial to identify the specific knowledge we need and establish measurable objectives. By planning the knowledge acquisition process and regularly reviewing our progress, we ensure that our goals remain relevant and adaptable to changing circumstances.

Given the overwhelming amount of information available, prioritization becomes essential in PKM. It helps us determine which knowledge is most relevant to our goals and enables us to focus our efforts on what matters most. Prioritization strategies can include ranking knowledge based on relevance, urgency, and impact on our personal and professional growth. Prioritizing can also be achieved by focusing on areas where there is a significant knowledge gap.

While goals provide us with direction, prioritization allows us to concentrate our efforts on what truly matters. By aligning our knowledge acquisition and organization with our objectives, we optimize our PKM practices and increase our chances of achieving desired outcomes.

To ensure that our PKM practices remain effective, it's important to regularly review and adjust our goals and priorities as circumstances change and we acquire new knowledge. This iterative process keeps our PKM practices relevant and ensures that we continue to make progress.

Setting goals and prioritizing in PKM can present challenges. Additionally, there's a risk of over-analyzing and getting stuck in a perpetual cycle of planning without taking action. Acknowledging these challenges is essential in developing effective PKM practices.

To overcome these challenges, it's helpful to start with broad goals and gradually narrow them down. Utilizing tools and technologies can also aid in prioritization, making the process more efficient. Finding a balance between thorough analysis and taking action is key to ensuring that we don't get caught in a cycle of overthinking.

In PKM, we unlock numerous benefits by setting clear goals and prioritizing them. Increased productivity, improved decision-making, and personal and professional growth are just a few of the advantages. These skills provide us with a competitive edge in the knowledge economy.

Thus, it is essential to understand the significance of goal setting and prioritization in PKM as they enhance our ability to collect, organise, and use knowledge efficiently, ultimately leading to personal and professional success.

Time and Task Management for Personal Knowledge Management

One needs to develop strategies for effectively consuming and retaining information, organizing and structuring knowledge resources, and allocating time in a way that supports ongoing learning and the synthesis of new insights. It needs a strategy that not only covers time management but also task management. Let's learn its implementation below.

Time Management:

Effective time management is crucial for personal knowledge management. By allocating time wisely, individuals can ensure they have dedicated periods for learning, researching, and reflecting on new information. This helps prevent information overload and allows for better retention and application of knowledge.

Task Management:

Implementing task management techniques can significantly improve personal knowledge management. Some effective strategies include:

1. Prioritizing tasks based on importance and urgency
2. Breaking down large projects into smaller, manageable tasks
3. Using to-do lists or task management apps to track progress
4. Setting realistic deadlines for completing tasks
5. Allocating specific time blocks for different types of activities

Thus, it is clear from above that establishing clear goals, prioritizing tasks, managing time effectively, and organizing your tasks are all crucial components of successful Personal Knowledge Management. These elements work together to boost your productivity and drive personal growth.

In the next chapter, let's learn about evaluation and assessment of personal knowledge management.

Action Points:

1. Define 1 PKM Goal: "Curate all project research in one place by July 30."
2. Time-Block Learning: Schedule 25 mins daily for knowledge review (use Pomodoro timer).
3. Prioritize with MoSCoW: Categorize tasks: Must do, Should do, Could do, Won't do.

7

Evaluation and Assessment of PKM

****

"Personal knowledge management is the key to unlocking your full potential." - ***David Allen***

Approaches to Evaluating PKM:

In a nutshell, you've got to assess your personal knowledge management game if you want to make the most of what you know and remember it for the long haul. But here's the deal, this assessment can't just be some half-assed effort. You've got to bring the thunder with a balanced and comprehensive approach. That means mixing it up with both qualitative and quantitative methods, and getting in the trenches with some usability testing and user feedback.

See, by throwing all these different evaluation strategies into the mix, you'll start to see the bigger picture of how personal knowledge management really works. But hold up, there's a catch. We've also got to be real about the criticisms and limitations of these strategies. No doubt, they've got their flaws. But hey, with a little planning and careful consideration of the specific context and objectives, we can totally address them.

We've got to keep pushing the envelope with further research and exploration of new evaluation approaches in personal knowledge management. That's how we're going to level up our knowledge management practices and score some killer educational outcomes. So let's get out there and make it happen!

Metrics and Indicators for Assessing Personal Knowledge Management:

Metrics and indicators are the holy grail when it comes to evaluating and measuring the effectiveness of personal knowledge management. They provide both quantitative and qualitative ways to assess all aspects of personal knowledge management. In this section, we're going to dive deep into the concept of metrics and indicators, why they matter, and how we can use them to evaluate personal knowledge management.

When it comes to personal knowledge management, one crucial aspect is acquiring new knowledge. We can use metrics to evaluate knowledge acquisition by looking at things like the number of new concepts learned, the depth of understanding achieved, and the rate at which knowledge is acquired. For example, we could measure the number of new books read or the number of hours spent in training sessions. These metrics help us understand how effective our personal knowledge management is at acquiring new knowledge.

But knowledge acquisition isn't worth a damn if we can't retain it. That's where **metrics** for assessing knowledge retention come into play. We can look at things like recall tests, the longevity of retained knowledge, and our ability to recall information from memory. For example, we could measure the percentage of information retained from a training session after a certain period of time. These metrics give us insights into how well we're retaining and recalling knowledge.

Now, what good is knowledge if we don't use it? Applying acquired knowledge is a crucial part of personal knowledge management. Metrics for assessing the application of knowledge can include performance in problem-solving tasks, completion of practical assignments, and our ability to use knowledge in new or novel situations. For example, we could measure the success rate of solving complex problems using the knowledge we've acquired. These metrics show us how effective our personal knowledge management is at applying knowledge to real-world situations.

But here's the kicker – personal knowledge management doesn't just impact our personal lives, it also has a direct effect on our professional growth. That's why **indicators** for evaluating this impact are essential. We can look at things like career advancements, job performance evaluations, and skill development. For example, we could measure the number of promotions or salary increases we achieve as a result of improved knowledge management. These indicators demonstrate the correlation between personal knowledge management and professional growth.

And let's not forget about decision-making. Our personal knowledge management plays a big role in how we make decisions. Metrics for assessing this impact can include decision accuracy, confidence in decision-making, and the speed at which decisions are made. For example, we could measure the percentage of decisions we make that result in positive outcomes. These metrics give us insights into how effective our personal knowledge management is in decision-making processes.

But wait, there's more! In order to compare and analyze all these metrics and indicators, statistical significance is crucial. We need to apply statistical analysis to determine the reliability and validity of the metrics we're using. By using techniques like correlation analysis or regression analysis, we can measure and compare the significance of these metrics.

Of course, it's not just about crunching numbers – interpreting these metrics and indicators is vital. We need to understand what they mean and how they reflect the effectiveness of our personal knowledge management. Proper interpretation allows us to make informed decisions and make adjustments to our knowledge management strategies.

Now, to be honest – there are challenges and limitations when it comes to using metrics and indicators for assessing personal knowledge management. Biases, inaccuracies, and variable factors can mess with the reliability and validity of our metrics. It's important to address these challenges and limitations to ensure the accuracy and effectiveness of our assessment.

But here's the kicker – the metrics and indicators we use for assessing personal knowledge management have huge implications for individuals, educators, and organizations. Understanding these implications can lead to improved personal knowledge management strategies and more effective educational practices. And, why stop there? We can also develop new and innovative metrics and indicators to take our assessments to the next level.

So, to wrap it all up – metrics and indicators are the bomb when it comes to assessing personal knowledge management. By evaluating knowledge acquisition, retention, application, impact on professional growth, and decision-making, we can gain insights into how effective our knowledge management strategies are. Understanding the statistical significance, interpreting the metrics, and addressing challenges and limitations only make our assessments more valid and reliable. The implications and potential future directions of these metrics and indicators offer exciting possibilities for improving our personal knowledge management practices.

Continuous Improvement and Iterative Evaluation in Personal Knowledge Management:

When it comes to personal knowledge management, embracing continuous improvement and iterative evaluation is key. These concepts are the foundation for learning and growth, allowing individuals to effectively manage their knowledge and enhance their understanding. By constantly seeking ways to improve existing knowledge and skills, as well as being open to new ideas and information, individuals can embark on a lifelong journey of learning and development.

Continuous improvement involves constantly seeking opportunities to enhance one's knowledge and skills. It requires individuals to be proactive in their learning, constantly seeking new insights and perspectives. By actively engaging in this process, individuals can deepen their understanding and retention of knowledge. For example, a librarian looking to improve their information literacy skills might attend relevant workshops, read scholarly articles, and seek guidance from experienced colleagues.

Iterative evaluation is a crucial component of personal knowledge management. It involves regularly assessing one's knowledge and understanding and making adjustments based on these assessments. Through iterative evaluation, individuals can identify gaps in their knowledge and actively work to fill them. This process encourages individuals to reflect on their learning journey, acknowledge areas for improvement, and make necessary adjustments to enhance their knowledge management practices.

Feedback loops play a crucial role in iterative evaluation. These loops involve taking action, reflecting on the outcomes, and making changes based on this reflection. For example, a library user may seek feedback from a librarian regarding their research skills. The librarian can then provide constructive feedback and suggest ways to improve their research techniques. By embracing feedback loops, individuals can effectively gauge their progress and make targeted improvements.

To create and use feedback loops in personal knowledge management, individuals can follow a structured approach. They can monitor their progress, gather feedback from mentors, peers, or experts in the field, reflect on the feedback received, and make necessary changes to their knowledge management practices. This iterative process ensures continuous improvement and enables individuals to refine their knowledge management strategies effectively.

Technology plays a significant role in supporting continuous improvement and iterative evaluation in personal knowledge management. Digital tools can help individuals track their progress, provide instant feedback, and facilitate learning through various platforms and applications. For example, knowledge management software can assist in organizing and retrieving information, while online learning platforms provide opportunities for continuous skill development.

While continuous improvement and iterative evaluation are essential in personal knowledge management, there can be potential challenges or barriers. Lack of time, resistance to change, and fear of failure are common obstacles. To overcome these challenges, individuals can set realistic goals, prioritize tasks effectively, and seek support from mentors or peers. Embracing these strategies as a lifelong journey rather than a one-time effort will enable individuals to navigate these challenges and continue to improve their knowledge management practices.

In the next chapter, let's learn how technology can assist in acquiring and delivering knowledge.

Action Points:

1. Track Retention: Test recall of last week's notes—grade accuracy (1-10).
2. Measure Output: Count how often you reference your PKM system daily. Aim for 5+ uses.
3. Seek Feedback: Ask a peer: "What's one way my knowledge-sharing could improve?"

8

PKM: Acquiring and Delivering Knowledge

****

"The goal of personal knowledge management is to turn information into action."
- Cal Newport

In this chapter, we will learn about two main components of PKM - knowledge acquisition and delivery - and their significance in the realm of knowledge seeker (or library users) and librarians.

Knowledge acquisition is the process of obtaining new information, skills, or expertise. It forms the bedrock of personal knowledge and is integral to PKM. Individuals acquire knowledge through various means, such as formal education, informal learning, and hands-on experience. Reading books, attending workshops, and engaging in conversations with experts are common methods of acquiring knowledge.

Recognizing the importance of knowledge acquisition is crucial for library users/librarians (as it helps to stay informed and provide accurate information to others).

In today's digital age, technology plays a vital role in knowledge acquisition. The internet, online databases, and social media platforms offer a wealth of information and resources. Guardians of knowledge can leverage these technologies to access a wide range of sources, including scholarly articles, e-books, and online courses. Platforms like YouTube, Khan Academy, and MOOCs (Massive Open Online Courses) enable individuals to acquire knowledge in various subjects at their convenience. Understanding and effectively utilizing these digital tools are essential for successful knowledge acquisition in PKM.

Effective knowledge acquisition necessitates a set of skills that enable individuals to critically evaluate, interpret, and apply the information they come across. Critical thinking, problem-solving, communication, and information literacy skills are paramount in acquiring knowledge effectively. For example, library users need to critically analyze sources and assess their credibility before incorporating them into their personal knowledge base. Librarians, on the other hand, require strong information literacy skills to guide users in navigating through the vast amount of information available and identifying reliable sources.

Knowledge Delivery

Knowledge acquisition and knowledge delivery are interconnected processes within PKM. Acquired knowledge needs to be transformed and effectively shared with others.

This transition ensures that the knowledge gained is not only retained but also disseminated to benefit others. Understanding this relationship is vital for library users and librarians as they not only acquire knowledge but also have a responsibility to deliver it to their communities.

Knowledge delivery involves various methods, such as teaching, mentoring, content creation (by writing books), and online sharing (to share acquired knowledge with others). Librarians may conduct workshops or training sessions to disseminate information and enhance the skills of library users. Content creators, such as bloggers or vloggers, deliver knowledge through their chosen platforms, reaching a wider audience.

Technology plays a significant role in facilitating knowledge delivery. Platforms like blogs, social media, and e-learning platforms provide accessible channels for individuals to share their knowledge with a global audience. Library users and librarians can leverage these technologies to create and disseminate content, engage with communities, and collaborate with others. For example, librarians can use social media platforms to share informative articles or organize online discussions, while library users can create blogs to document their personal knowledge journeys (or the knowledge insights they gain can also be shared with others).

Effective knowledge delivery requires a set of skills that enable individuals to communicate their knowledge effectively and engage with their audience. Strong communication skills, pedagogical skills, content creation skills, and digital literacy are crucial for delivering knowledge successfully. For example, librarians need to communicate complex concepts in a way that is understandable to different user groups, while content creators need to craft engaging and informative content to capture their audience's attention. Developing these skills enhances the impact of knowledge delivery in PKM.

Cultural context also plays a significant role in both acquiring and delivering knowledge. Cultural norms, values, and languages can influence the way individuals manage their personal knowledge. For example, library users and librarians serving diverse communities need to consider cultural sensitivities and adapt their knowledge acquisition and delivery strategies accordingly. Understanding the importance of cultural context ensures that knowledge is shared in a meaningful and inclusive manner.

Managing personal knowledge presents its own set of challenges. Information overload, the digital divide, and privacy concerns are common obstacles that individuals face in the PKM process. Library users and librarians need to be aware of these challenges and develop strategies to overcome them. For instance, effective information filtering techniques, promoting digital literacy, and ensuring privacy protection are some solutions that can be implemented. By addressing these challenges, individuals can optimize their PKM processes and enhance their overall knowledge management capabilities.

It is clear from above that knowledge acquisition and delivery are two sides of the same coin in the journey of lifelong learning and effective communication. By embracing and implementing these principles, individuals can enhance their knowledge management abilities and make meaningful contributions to their communities/society.

In the next chapter, let's learn about personalized learning and adaptive systems in personal knowledge management.

Actions Points:

1. Teach Back: Explain a new concept you learned to a colleague within 48 hours.
2. Curate a "Top 3" List: Share 3 best resources on a topic via email/blog.
3. Practice Active Note-Taking: Next meeting, use Cornell Method (summary + action column).

9

Personalized Learning and Adaptive System in PKM

****

"The more you know, the more you know you don't know." - ***Aristotle***

Personalized learning and adaptive systems have become essential for optimizing our learning experiences in PKM. These innovative approaches cater to our individual needs and preferences, offering tailored experiences that optimize our acquisition and retention of knowledge.

Personalized learning recognizes that each of us is unique and has our own specific preferences and needs when it comes to learning. By customizing our learning experiences, it fosters effective personal knowledge management. This can involve delivering content that is tailored to our interests and abilities, as well as utilizing adaptive assessments that adjust to our individual strengths and weaknesses. Ultimately, personalized learning empowers us to take ownership of our own knowledge acquisition journey.

Learning analytics plays a vital role in the realm of personalized learning by leveraging data to gain insight into our behaviors and needs as learners. By collecting and analyzing data related to our interactions, learning analytics can identify patterns and preferences, ultimately enabling more personalized learning experiences. It also helps identify our strengths and weaknesses, allowing for targeted resources that can further enhance our development.

Adaptive systems are another game-changer in personal knowledge management. These systems adjust to our individual knowledge levels, learning pace, and preferences, utilizing sophisticated algorithms and artificial intelligence to provide personalized recommendations and feedback. By adapting the difficulty of content and suggesting supplementary resources, adaptive systems optimize engagement and retention.

The benefits of adaptive systems in personal knowledge management are numerous. They enhance learning efficiency by eliminating redundant content and promote engagement through interactive experiences. Additionally, they improve retention by reinforcing key concepts based on our individual performance.

To truly maximize our personal knowledge management, it is advantageous to integrate personalized learning and adaptive systems. By combining these approaches, we can experience tailored content delivery while harnessing the adaptability and intelligence of technology. Online platforms can recommend personalized resources based on our progress and interests, ensuring that we are consistently discovering relevant knowledge aligned with our needs.

Personalized recommendations are a powerful tool in aiding individuals in their quest of knowledge. These recommendations are based on our interests and past interactions, and are generated through algorithms and machine learning. They can suggest books, articles, videos, and other resources that are specifically tailored to our needs, enabling us to explore topics that align with our interests and goals.

Cortana (a personal productivity assistant of Microsoft), for example, offers tailored experiences, monitors user progress, and dynamically changes content to meet an individual's needs through adaptive learning technologies. By utilizing adaptive algorithms and analytics, they can deliver tailored content and assessments, monitor our interactions, and provide real-time feedback. This empowers us to optimize our personal knowledge management in a way that suits our unique needs and learning style.

However, it is important to acknowledge that personalized learning and adaptive systems also face challenges. Data privacy is a significant concern, as protecting and ethically using learner data must be a top priority. Additionally, over-personalization can potentially limit our exposure to diverse perspectives, which is vital for a well-rounded education. Implementation of these systems can also be complex and resource-intensive, requiring a robust infrastructure and adequate training.

Despite these challenges, it is clear that personalized learning and adaptive systems have significant implications for personal knowledge management. They are revolutionizing the way we acquire, organize, and manage knowledge, empowering us to take ownership of our learning journey. As technology continues to advance, these approaches enhance accessibility, flexibility, and effectiveness in personal knowledge management, promising more personalized and impactful learning experiences.

Next chapter is the heart of this book and that will help you take your personal knowledge management journey to the next level. Let's learn how?

Action Points:

1. Activate AI Assistance: Use ChatGPT/Claude to summarize one complex article.
2. Try Adaptive Learning: Complete one module on Khan Academy/Coursera; note how content adjusts to your pace.
3. Audit Algorithms: Review YouTube/Netflix recommendations. Save one valuable suggestion to your PKM.

10

Building a Second Brain

****

"Creativity is just connecting things." - ***Steve Jobs***

The idea of "Building a Second Brain" is a framework for managing knowledge in a way that enhances creativity, productivity, and learning. A "second brain" refers to a system or method—typically digital—designed to capture, organize, and retrieve ideas and insights when needed. This chapter explores three powerful concepts that contribute to this process: digital gardens, the Zettelkasten method, and personal wikis.

The Concept of Digital Gardens:

A digital garden is a personal and evolving repository of knowledge. Unlike blogs or traditional note-taking, which often emphasize linearity or chronology, digital gardens are designed to be organic, non-linear, and interconnected. Picture a literal garden in which you plant seeds that represent your ideas, nurturing and cultivating them over time as they grow and develop. In this metaphorical garden, some ideas flourish and transform into towering trees, symbolizing well-developed concepts that stand tall and strong. Meanwhile, other ideas may remain as smaller plants, patiently awaiting the right conditions or connections to thrive and fully blossom. This dynamic environment allows for the continuous growth and evolution of knowledge, as new ideas can intertwine with existing ones, creating a rich tapestry of interconnected thoughts. Just as a physical garden requires care, attention, and time to reach its potential, a digital garden also demands ongoing nurturing and exploration to truly reflect the depth and breadth of one's intellectual journey.

Key Characteristics of Digital Gardens

1. Evolution Over Time: Digital gardens evolve as you gain more knowledge and refine your understanding. Old ideas are revisited, updated, or pruned, reflecting your growth and learning.

2. Interconnected Notes: Notes in a digital garden are not isolated. They are linked to each other, creating a web of connections that mirrors how our minds work. This interconnectedness helps in discovering patterns and sparking creativity.

3. Public or Private: Digital gardens can be either public-facing, allowing others to engage with and learn from your notes, or private, serving as a personal thinking space. Many creators opt for a mix, sharing some insights while keeping others private.

4.Tool-Agnostic: Tools like Obsidian, Roam Research, or Notion are popular for creating digital gardens. The choice of tool matters less than the principles of organization and growth.

Why Build a Digital Garden?

Clarity: By regularly organizing and revising your thoughts, you gain clarity and deepen your understanding.

Creativity: The non-linear structure allows for unexpected connections between ideas.

Legacy: If shared publicly, your digital garden can serve as a resource for others, contributing to a broader community of learning.

Creating your digital garden is as simple as starting with a handful of notes and ensuring they are interconnected. Over time, it becomes a vibrant ecosystem of ideas, insights, and inspirations.

The Zettelkasten Method

The Zettelkasten method is a systematic approach to note-taking that originated with German sociologist Niklas Luhmann. His "slip-box" method allowed him to produce over 70 books and 400 articles during his lifetime. The Zettelkasten method is especially useful for those engaged in research, writing, or any intellectual work requiring deep, interconnected thought.

Core Principles of Zettelkasten

1. **Atomic Notes:** Each note captures a single idea or concept. Keeping notes atomic ensures clarity and prevents ideas from being buried within lengthy texts.

2. **Unique Identifiers:** Every note is given a unique identifier, which could be a combination of numbers, dates, or alphanumeric codes. This makes it easy to reference and link notes.

3. **Interconnectedness:** Notes are linked to each other based on themes, ideas, or contexts. For example, a note about "decision-making" might link to one about "cognitive biases."

4. **Emergence of Structure:** Unlike traditional methods where structure is imposed from the start, Zettelkasten al-

lows structure to emerge naturally through connections between notes. This mirrors the organic way our minds work.

How to Implement the Zettelkasten Method

1. **Capture Notes:** Start by writing down ideas as you encounter them. Each idea should be clear, concise, and contained within a single note.

2. **Link Notes:** Whenever you add a note, think about how it connects to existing notes. Use hyperlinks if you're using digital tools.

3. **Review Regularly:** Periodically revisit your notes to refine, expand, or connect them further. This process solidifies your understanding and keeps your system dynamic.

Tools for Zettelkasten: Several digital tools can facilitate the Zettelkasten method:

- **Obsidian:** Its graph view makes it easy to visualize connections between notes.
- **Roam Research:** Focuses on bi-directional linking, ideal for creating a web of ideas.
- Notion: While not specifically designed for Zettelkasten, its database features can be adapted for this method.

By using the Zettelkasten method, you transform note-taking from a passive activity into an active, creative process that fuels learning and insight.

Creating a Personal Wiki

A personal wiki is a customizable digital knowledge base that serves as a hub for your thoughts, projects, and resources. Inspired by public wikis like Wikipedia, a personal wiki allows you to create pages and link them to build a structured yet flexible repository of knowledge.

Why Create a Personal Wiki?

1. **Centralized Knowledge:** A personal wiki consolidates scattered notes, ideas, and references into one accessible location.

2. **Customizable Structure:** Unlike rigid organizational systems, a wiki allows you to structure your knowledge in a way that aligns with your thinking process.

3. **Versatility:** Personal wikis can be used for everything from project management and goal tracking to storing ideas and research notes.

Steps to Build a Personal Wiki

1. **Choose a Tool:** Several tools can help you build a personal wiki, such as Notion, TiddlyWiki, or Obsidian. Choose one that fits your preferences and workflow.

2. **Define Key Categories:** Start by creating broad categories like "Work Projects," "Learning," "Personal Development," or "Hobbies." These will serve as the main branches of your wiki.

3. **Create and Link Pages:** Each page in your wiki should focus on a single topic. Link related pages to create a web of connections, making it easier to navigate and discover related information.

4. **Add Context and Media:** Enhance your wiki pages with images, videos, or links to external resources. This makes your knowledge base richer and more engaging.

Best Practices for Maintaining a Personal Wiki

- **Keep It Updated:** Regularly review and update your wiki to ensure it remains relevant and useful.
- **Focus on Usability:** Use clear titles and consistent formatting to make your wiki easy to navigate.
- **Integrate with Other Tools:** Link your wiki to other tools like calendars or task managers to create a seamless productivity system.

By building a personal wiki, you create a second brain that is not only a repository of knowledge but also a tool for creativity, problem-solving, and productivity.

Bringing It All Together

The concepts of digital gardens, the Zettelkasten method, and personal wikis are not mutually exclusive rather, they are inherently interconnected:

- A digital garden captures your evolving ideas and fosters creativity.
- The Zettelkasten method adds rigor and interconnectedness to your notes.
- A personal wiki organizes your knowledge into a centralized, user-friendly system.

By integrating these approaches, you can build a second brain tailored to your unique needs and goals. This second brain not only enhances your ability to think and learn but also serves as a source of inspiration and productivity for years to come.

In our fast-paced, information-driven world, having a reliable system to manage knowledge is no longer a luxury—it's a necessity. Start small, stay consistent, and watch as your second brain grows into a powerful ally in your personal and professional life.

Next, let's examine how personal knowledge management will influence the future of libraries in the following chapter.

Action Points:

1. Plant a "Digital Seed": Create 3 atomic notes in Obsidian/Roam (1 idea per note). Link 2 notes.
2. Build a Zettelkasten ID: Assign a unique tag (e.g., 20250715-MKTG) to today's key insight.
3. Map Your Garden: Sketch connections between 5 ideas using a free mind-mapping tool (Miro/MindMeister).

11

PKM and the Future of Libraries

****

*"Personal knowledge is a garden; tend it daily, and watch it grow." - **Unknown***

Libraries have undergone a remarkable transformation from dusty book repositories to vibrant hubs that foster the creation and management of knowledge. In this digital era, libraries have taken on a crucial role in developing the indispensable skills of digital and information literacy, which are essential for effective personal knowledge management. Digital literacy, encompassing the ability to navigate, utilize, and critically evaluate digital technologies, goes hand in hand with information literacy, which involves the skills required to find, assess, and effectively employ information. This chapter delves into how libraries cultivate these vital skills and highlights their significance in personal knowledge management.

One shining example of a library that has successfully implemented initiatives to promote digital and information literacy is the illustrious New Horizons Library. Recognizing the imperative to equip library users with these indispensable skills, the library launched a comprehensive program aimed at enhancing digital and information literacy.

The digital literacy initiative of the New Horizons Library primarily focuses on providing users with the necessary resources and training opportunities to develop their digital prowess. Workshops on a wide array of topics such as internet safety, online research, and digital content creation are offered. Additionally, the library provides online courses and tutorial sessions, allowing users to learn at their own pace. The response from library users has been overwhelmingly positive, with many expressing profound gratitude for the invaluable resources and support.

Simultaneously, the library's information literacy initiative endeavors to equip users with the skills needed to locate and evaluate reliable information. Training programs have been developed to teach users how to navigate databases, identify credible sources, and avoid plagiarism. Furthermore, the library offers literacy guides and online resources to assist users in enhancing their research skills. The impact of these initiatives has been palpable, as library users report feeling more confident and competent in their ability to find and effectively employ information.

To bolster these initiatives, the New Horizons Library has established strategic partnerships with various stakeholders. Collaborations with local schools have been forged, ensuring the integration of digital and information literacy into the curriculum and providing students with a solid foundation in these essential skills. The library also works closely with community organizations and tech companies, offering specialized training programs and granting access to cutting-edge technologies. These partnerships have significantly expanded the reach and impact of the library's initiatives.

One remarkable success story stemming from the New Horizons Library is that of Sarah, a college student who initially grappled with digital and information literacy skills. Through the library's workshops and training programs, Sarah developed the ability to critically evaluate online information and skillfully utilize digital tools for research. This newfound skill set had a profound impact on Sarah's personal knowledge management, enabling her to excel in her studies and make well-informed decisions in her personal life.

Implementing these initiatives did not come without challenges, as the library encountered budget constraints that limited their ability to invest in technology and resources. Additionally, there was a shortage of skilled staff members capable of effectively imparting digital and information literacy skills. Some library users also expressed resistance, feeling overwhelmed by the rapid pace of technological advancements. However, the library remained steadfast in its commitment to overcoming these challenges and ensuring the success of their programs.

To surmount these obstacles, the New Horizons Library implemented an array of solutions and strategies. Active fundraising efforts were undertaken to secure additional funding for technology upgrades and resource development. Staff members underwent training programs to enhance their own digital and information literacy skills, equipping them to better support library users. The library also engaged users through interactive activities and competitions, fostering a sense of excitement and motivation to learn.

Looking to the future, libraries will continue to play a pivotal role in promoting digital and information literacy skills. As technology continues to advance, libraries must adapt and expand their offerings to meet the ever-evolving needs of users. Exploring partnerships with emerging technology companies, developing new online courses, and providing support for burgeoning technologies like virtual reality (VR) and artificial intelligence (AI) are just a few avenues that libraries can explore. By seizing these opportunities, libraries will remain invaluable resources for cultivating the vital skills necessary for effective personal knowledge management in this digital age.

In conclusion, libraries occupy a significant position in cultivating digital and information literacy skills. Through initiatives like the New Horizons Library's comprehensive program, libraries can furnish users with the necessary resources, training, and support to enhance their digital and information literacy skills. Real-world examples and success stories serve as testament to the positive impact these initiatives have on personal knowledge management. While challenges may arise, libraries possess the ability to overcome them through innovative solutions and strategies. As the digital landscape continues to evolve, libraries must adapt and expand their offerings to ensure their continued relevance and their capacity to empower users with the skills they need for effective personal knowledge management.

Let's discuss about the future trends in personal knowledge management space in the next chapter.

Action Points:

1. Visit a Library/Online Archive: Explore one digital resource (e.g., Internet Archive). Save 2 finds.
2. Boost Digital Literacy: Watch one tutorial on verifying online sources (e.g., MediaWise).
3. Share a Resource: Recommend a free learning platform (e.g., Libby, Project Gutenberg) to a friend.

12

Future Trends in PKM

****

"Your mind is a library. Be its best librarian." - ***Unknown***

With increasing volumes of data and the need for real-time access to relevant information, PKM systems must adapt to meet changing demands. Emerging technologies, such as artificial intelligence (AI), augmented reality (AR), and spatial computing, are poised to redefine how we interact with and utilize knowledge. This chapter delves into these key areas and offers predictions on the evolution of PKM in the coming years.

1. **Artificial Intelligence and PKM:** Artificial intelligence has already begun transforming PKM, but its future potential is even more profound. As we look ahead, innovations driven by AI will not only improve the methods we use to collect and store vast amounts of information but also revolutionize the ways we retrieve and apply that

knowledge. This transformation will lead to a more seamless and personalized experience, allowing individuals to interact with their knowledge in ways that are much more intuitive and effective. As AI continues to develop, the possibilities for enhancing PKM practices will expand, creating tools and systems that tailor to individual needs while augmenting our ability to learn and grow throughout our lives.

a. Automating Knowledge Organization

AI excels in handling repetitive and labor-intensive tasks. In PKM, this means:

- Automatic Categorization: AI can classify and tag notes, documents, and media based on their content and context without user input.
- Intelligent Sorting: By understanding user preferences and habits, AI can prioritize information, ensuring the most relevant data is always at hand.
- Dynamic Knowledge Graphs: AI will create interconnected knowledge maps, identifying links between seemingly unrelated topics to foster deeper understanding.

b. Enhanced Information Retrieval

Future PKM tools will leverage AI for advanced search capabilities:

- Context-Aware Queries: Instead of relying solely on keywords, AI will analyze the context of user queries to deliver precise results. For instance, asking, "What were my insights on productivity tools from last year?" could retrieve related notes, articles, and summaries.

• Natural Language Processing (NLP): NLP advancements will enable users to interact with their PKM systems conversationally, asking questions or making requests in plain language.

c. Personalized Learning and Growth

AI will enable users to tailor their PKM systems to their unique goals and learning paths in the following manner:

• Skill Development: By analyzing gaps in knowledge, AI can recommend resources, courses, or exercises to help users build expertise in targeted areas.

• Predictive Assistance: AI could anticipate future information needs based on projects, interests, or professional trends, delivering curated recommendations proactively.

d. Collaboration and Knowledge Sharing

AI can also facilitate collaborative knowledge management:

• Summarization Tools: AI is already condensing long documents, meeting notes, or research papers into actionable insights, making information sharing more efficient.

• Real-time Translation: Breaking down language barriers, AI-powered translation will make global collaboration seamless, enabling the exchange of knowledge across cultures.

2. Augmented Reality and Spatial Computing: Augmented reality (AR) and spatial computing are set to revolutionize how we interact with information by making it more immersive, intuitive, and context-aware. These technologies will transform PKM into an embodied experience, allowing users to visualize and manipulate their knowledge in real-time.

a. Immersive Knowledge Visualization

Spatial computing will enable users to interact with their knowledge in three-dimensional environments:

• Virtual Knowledge Maps: Instead of scrolling through lists or folders, users can navigate their notes, documents, and ideas in a 3D space. For example, a researcher could visually organize key themes of a project as floating nodes in a virtual room.

• Dynamic Dashboards: AR could project real-time data and insights onto physical surfaces, allowing for intuitive interactions. Imagine a student using AR glasses to see lecture notes and related references displayed in their study area.

b. Seamless Knowledge Capture

AR will make capturing knowledge from the physical world more intuitive:

• Real-time Annotations: Users can overlay digital notes or highlights on physical objects or spaces. For instance, while visiting a museum, an AR device could capture observations and attach them to specific exhibits.

• Contextual Tagging: Spatial computing systems could automatically tag knowledge based on location or environment, creating richer metadata for future retrieval.

c. Enhanced Collaboration in Virtual Spaces

AR and spatial computing will redefine collaborative knowledge management:

• Shared AR Workspaces: Teams could brainstorm in virtual environments, visualizing and building upon each other's ideas in real-time, regardless of physical location.

• Interactive Training Modules: PKM tools integrated with AR could provide hands-on learning experiences. For example, a technician might use AR to overlay repair instructions onto machinery, with the system recording and storing these steps for future reference.

d. Accessibility and Inclusivity

AR will make PKM more accessible by accommodating diverse user needs:

• Voice and Gesture Controls: These interfaces will allow individuals with physical disabilities to interact with their knowledge systems effortlessly.

• Real-time Transcriptions: AR devices could transcribe conversations or lectures into digital formats, enabling users to capture and store valuable information instantly.

3. Predictions for the Evolution of PKM: The interplay of AI, AR, and other emerging technologies suggests a future where PKM is more intelligent, intuitive, and indispensable. Below are some key predictions for how PKM will evolve:

a. Greater Personalization

PKM systems will adapt dynamically to individual preferences, goals, and behaviors:

- Adaptive Interfaces: Future systems will modify layouts, features, and workflows based on user habits, ensuring a personalized experience.
- Goal-Oriented Knowledge Management: Tools will prioritize and present information that aligns with personal or professional objectives, such as learning a new language or preparing for a specific project.

b. Decentralized Knowledge Ecosystems

As privacy concerns grow, PKM systems will shift towards decentralized models:

- Blockchain Integration: Blockchain technology could enable users to own and control their knowledge assets securely, ensuring data integrity and privacy.
- Open Standards: Interoperability between PKM tools will allow users to switch platforms or integrate multiple systems seamlessly.

c. Emotional and Contextual Awareness

Future PKM systems will account for the user's emotional state and situational context:

- Mood-Based Curation: AI could adjust the type and presentation of information based on detected mood, offering lighter content during stressful times or in-depth resources when users feel focused.

• Environmental Adaptation: Context-aware PKM tools could tailor workflows based on location, time of day, or activity. For example, a system might prioritize casual reading suggestions during a commute and work-related tasks in an office setting.

d. Continuous Learning and Evolution

PKM tools will evolve alongside users, offering features that grow with their needs:

• Lifelong Learning Companion: These systems will track progress over years, providing insights into personal growth and areas for improvement.

• Knowledge Retention Strategies: AI will help combat forgetting by using spaced repetition techniques, prompting users to revisit key information at optimal intervals.

e. Fusion of Work and Personal Knowledge

As work-life boundaries blur, PKM systems will unify professional and personal knowledge:

• Unified Dashboards: Future tools will consolidate tasks, goals, and resources, offering a holistic view of priorities.

• Intelligent Compartmentalization: Systems will maintain boundaries when needed, ensuring that work-related data doesn't overwhelm personal projects or vice versa.

Let's summarize this chapter here: The future of Personal Knowledge Management lies in the seamless integration of advanced technologies like artificial intelligence, augmented reality, and spatial computing. These innovations will make PKM systems smarter, more intuitive, and deeply embedded in our daily lives. By personalizing experiences, enhancing collaboration, and offering immersive interactions, these tools will empower individuals to navigate the complexities of the information age with confidence and creativity. As PKM continues to evolve, it promises to not only manage knowledge but also unlock the full potential of human intelligence.

It's just a glimpse, and there may be more than this.

Action Points:

1. Test an AI Tool: Use Gemini/Perplexity to generate a research summary. Compare to your notes.
2. Imagine AR: Sketch how spatial computing could visualize your PKM (e.g., 3D knowledge tree).
3. Future-Proof Your System: Export notes from one app to plain text files (future-proofing).

13

Conclusions

****

"Nothing will work unless you do." - ***Maya Angelou***

This book has provided a comprehensive guide to personal knowledge management, emphasizing its importance in navigating the complexities of the information age. By understanding the foundations of PKM, utilizing effective tools and strategies, and embracing future trends, individuals can enhance their ability to manage knowledge effectively.

The journey of personal knowledge management is inherently a personal one; it is not simply a one-size-fits-all process, but rather one that requires ongoing improvement, reflection, and adaptation to address diverse individual needs, preferences, and goals. As the landscape of technology continues to evolve at a rapid pace, individuals must remain vigilant and open to adopting new methodologies that can aid in their quest for knowledge mastery. This approach leverages human intelligence and creativity, providing opportunities for individuals to explore their potential and achieve their aspirations in a dynamic world.

In conclusion, "How to Manage Your Personal Knowledge: Wisdom for Creating a Second Brain" serves as a comprehensive guide for anyone seeking to take control of their knowledge in an information-rich environment. By adopting the principles and strategies outlined in this book, individuals can cultivate a robust PKM system that empowers them to thrive in both their personal and professional lives, ultimately unlocking their full potential in the knowledge economy.

Action Points:

1. Schedule Quarterly PKM Review: Block calendar time for system refinement.
2. Share Your Journey: Post one PKM win on social media with #SecondBrain.
3. Gift Knowledge: Donate this book to a library or colleague.

14

About the Author

Academic and Corporate Experience: Mr. Jadhav has over 20 years of professional experience, having worked extensively in both academic institutions and corporate organizations. His academic journey includes notable positions at the University of Mumbai, Thakur Polytechnic, and Usha Pravin Gandhi College of Management. On the corporate front, he has gained significant experience through his roles at Ocean Diving Centre and Tushar Desai Associates. This diverse blend of academic and corporate exposure has equipped him with a comprehensive perspective and expertise in both educational and business domains.

Teaching and Session Experience: Mr. Jadhav has delivered more than 225 sessions across a range of HRDC Centres, academic institutions, and corporate settings. His expertise is highly valued by teaching faculty, students, and LIS professionals alike.

Academic Qualifications: Mr. Jadhav holds a master's degree in library and information science (LIS) from Mumbai University, where he ranked 2nd in his batch. He also qualified for the 2017 UGC NET Exam in Library & Information Science. In addition, he completed a Post Graduate Diploma in Library and Information Management (PGDLIM) from the Tata Institute of Social Sciences (TISS) and holds a certification in Intellectual Property Rights (IPR).

Key Positions and Memberships:

- External Industry Expert: Internal Quality Assurance Cell (IQAC) at K G Law College (SNDT University)
- Member: College Development Committee at K G Law College (SNDT University)
- Member: Knowledge Resource Centre (KRC) of SNDT Women's University, Mumbai
- Member: Board of Studies for Library and Information Science at KG Joshi Bedekar College
- Joint Secretary: Bombay Science Library Association (BOSLA) for 2023–26
- Guest Faculty: Library and Information Science at Yashwantrao Chavan Maharashtra Open University (YCMOU)
- External Examiner: YCMOU Thane Branch, Joshi Bedekar College, Thane

9 789334 321326

Printed at Repro India Ltd.